To all parents and guardians – Your love, guidance, and patience shape the future. This book is for you, as you help children navigate the digital world safely and wisely.

Table of Content

Introduction

The digital world has transformed how we live, learn, and interact. For parents, this new era presents both incredible opportunities and unprecedented challenges. While technology can enhance education, foster creativity, and connect us with others, it also introduces risks that must be carefully managed—especially for children. This book serves as a practical guide to help you navigate the complexities of digital parenting, equipping you with the knowledge and strategies needed to protect and empower your child in the online world.

The Digital Age: A New Parenting Challenge

The way children engage with technology today is vastly different from previous generations. Kids are growing up in an era where digital devices are woven into every aspect of daily life—whether for school, entertainment, or socializing. Unlike the past, where technology was mainly limited to television and home computers, today's children have access to smartphones, tablets, gaming consoles, and smart devices that connect them to the internet at all times.

While technology offers many benefits, it also presents new challenges for parents. Unlike traditional parenting, which primarily focused on physical safety and personal behavior, digital parenting requires an understanding of cyber risks, online etiquette, and the ever-changing landscape of internet platforms. Many parents feel overwhelmed by the rapid pace of technological advancements and struggle to keep up with their children's digital lives.

One of the biggest challenges is that children often become familiar with new apps, games, and online trends much faster than their parents. This knowledge gap can make it difficult for parents to guide their children safely. Furthermore, online interactions are not always easy to monitor, and the potential risks—including cyberbullying, exposure to inappropriate content, and online predators—are more hidden than traditional dangers.

However, digital parenting does not mean banning technology or constantly spying on your child's activities. Instead, it involves learning how to create a safe and balanced digital environment, teaching responsible online behavior, and fostering open communication about internet use. This book will guide you through the essential steps to achieve that balance, ensuring that your child benefits from technology without falling into its pitfalls.

Why Digital Parenting Matters

You may wonder: *Is digital parenting really necessary? Can't kids just figure things out on their own?* The answer is simple—children need guidance in the digital world just as much as they do in the real world. The internet is vast and unfiltered, and without proper guidance, children may be exposed to harmful content or engage in risky behaviors.

Digital parenting matters because the online world is not always a safe place. Unlike a physical playground, where parents can see potential dangers and intervene when necessary, the internet is filled with invisible threats that can impact a child's mental, emotional, and even physical well-being. Without proper supervision, children may accidentally share personal information, become targets of cyberbullying, or develop unhealthy screen habits that affect their social skills and mental health.

Additionally, the way children use technology today will shape their future. Digital skills are essential in modern education and careers, but so is knowing how to use technology responsibly. By setting the right foundation, you can help your child develop a healthy relationship with technology—one that promotes learning, creativity, and safe interactions.

Understanding the Online World Your Child Navigates

To effectively guide your child, it's crucial to understand the digital world they are growing up in. The internet is more than just a tool—it's an entire ecosystem of apps, social networks, games, and virtual communities where children interact daily.

Children and teenagers use the internet for various reasons, including:

- **Social media** – Platforms like TikTok, Instagram, Snapchat, and Discord allow them to communicate with friends, share content, and follow influencers.
- **Gaming** – Online multiplayer games like Roblox, Fortnite, and Minecraft create digital spaces where children can interact with strangers and teammates.
- **Entertainment** – Video streaming platforms like YouTube and Netflix offer endless content, but not all of it is age-appropriate.
- **Education** – Online learning resources, virtual classrooms, and digital homework platforms are essential for modern education.

While each of these activities can be positive, they also come with risks. Social media can expose children to cyberbullying and unrealistic beauty standards. Online gaming can lead to interactions with strangers, and unrestricted internet access can result in exposure to inappropriate content. Understanding these digital spaces will help you set realistic boundaries and ensure your child's safety.

Common Cyber Threats and Risks

The internet is not just a source of entertainment and learning; it also comes with significant dangers that parents must be aware of. Some of the most common risks include:

1. Cyberbullying

Cyberbullying occurs when children use digital platforms to harass, threaten, or embarrass others. Unlike traditional bullying, online harassment can be anonymous and persistent, making it harder to escape.

2. Online Predators

Predators use online platforms to befriend children and gain their trust before attempting to exploit them. They may pretend to be someone they're not, gradually manipulating children into sharing personal information or inappropriate images.

3. Privacy Risks

Children may unknowingly share personal details online, such as their full name, school, or location, making them vulnerable to identity theft or unwanted contact from strangers.

4. Exposure to Inappropriate Content

The internet contains vast amounts of unfiltered content, including violence, hate speech, and adult material. Without proper restrictions, children can easily stumble upon harmful content.

5. Scams and Phishing Attacks

Children are often targeted by scammers who trick them into sharing account passwords or financial details through fake giveaways, phishing emails, or fraudulent apps.

These risks highlight why parental involvement in digital activities is crucial. By being proactive, parents can prevent potential dangers and educate children on how to navigate the online world safely.

How to Use This Book: A Step-by-Step Guide

This book is designed to be a **comprehensive yet practical** guide for parents of children at all ages. Whether you are new to digital parenting or already familiar with some aspects of online safety, this book provides clear, actionable steps to help you protect your child in the digital world.

Each section of the book is structured to provide:

- **Easy-to-understand explanations** of digital risks and trends.
- **Step-by-step strategies** for setting up parental controls, monitoring online activity, and creating family internet rules.
- **Practical tips** for teaching your child about online safety in a way that builds trust and responsibility.
- **Real-life examples** and scenarios to help you apply the lessons in everyday situations.

By following the guidance in this book, you will:

- Understand the latest online trends and risks.
- Learn how to set up parental controls on various devices.
- Teach your child how to stay safe and responsible online.

- Create a balanced approach to screen time and technology use.

The goal of this book is **not** to make technology seem dangerous or overwhelming but to empower you with the knowledge and tools to guide your child through the digital world safely. Digital parenting is not about banning devices—it's about creating a safe and positive digital environment where children can learn, grow, and thrive.

Let's embark on this journey together, ensuring that your child can navigate the digital age with confidence and security.

Part 1: Understanding the Online World

Chapter 1: The Digital Landscape for Kids

The Rise of the Internet and Social Media

The internet has transformed the way we live, work, and communicate. What started as a tool for researchers and businesses has now become a global necessity for people of all ages. Over the past few decades, the rise of the internet has been rapid, reshaping how information is accessed, entertainment is consumed, and social interactions take place.

For children and teenagers, the internet is an integral part of their daily lives. Unlike previous generations who grew up with limited access to digital devices, today's youth are surrounded by technology from an early age. Social media, in particular, has revolutionized communication, allowing kids to connect with peers, share their thoughts, and explore content beyond their immediate surroundings.

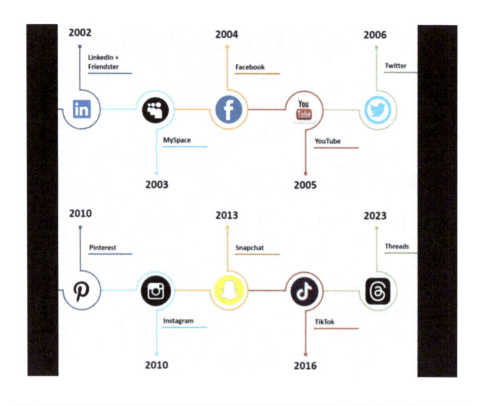

How Social Media Became So Popular

Social media platforms gained popularity due to their ability to offer instant connectivity, entertainment, and a sense of belonging. Platforms like Facebook, Instagram, Snapchat, TikTok, and YouTube provide children and teens with spaces to express themselves, follow trends, and interact with a broader community. With the convenience of smartphones, access to these platforms has become easier than ever, making social media an unavoidable part of childhood and adolescence.

However, while social media has many benefits, it also introduces significant risks. The way children interact with digital platforms shapes their social behavior, mental well-being, and perception of the world. As a parent or guardian, understanding the evolution of the internet and social media is the first step in guiding children toward responsible digital habits.

How Kids and Teens Use Technology Today

Technology is no longer just a tool for learning and entertainment; it has become a lifestyle. Children and teenagers use digital devices in diverse ways, influencing their education, social life, and even personal development. Understanding how they engage with technology can help parents set appropriate boundaries and ensure a balanced digital experience.

Education and Learning

One of the biggest benefits of technology is its role in education. Schools integrate digital tools like online classrooms, educational apps, and research platforms to enhance learning experiences. Many students use tablets, laptops, and smartphones to complete assignments, attend virtual classes, or watch instructional videos on platforms like YouTube and Khan Academy.

Entertainment and Streaming

Streaming services have replaced traditional television for many young users. Platforms like Netflix, Disney+, and YouTube allow children to watch their favorite shows and movies on demand. YouTube, in particular, is widely popular among kids for its variety of content, including cartoons, educational videos, DIY projects, and video game streams.

Gaming and Online Play

Video games have evolved beyond single-player experiences, becoming highly interactive social platforms. Online games such as Fortnite, Roblox, Minecraft, and Among Us allow children to connect with friends and strangers, communicate via voice or text chat, and engage in immersive digital worlds. While gaming can be a fun and even educational activity, it also comes with concerns such as addiction, online predators, and exposure to inappropriate content.

Social Media and Messaging

Social media is the primary communication tool for many teenagers. Apps like Snapchat, Instagram, TikTok, and WhatsApp allow them to share photos, videos, and messages instantly. These platforms enable kids to build friendships and stay updated on trends, but they also expose them to issues such as cyberbullying, privacy risks, and unrealistic beauty standards.

Shopping and Online Transactions

Many children and teens are becoming digital consumers, purchasing virtual items in games, ordering products online, or subscribing to streaming services. Without proper supervision, they may fall victim to scams, unauthorized purchases, or phishing attacks designed to steal personal information.

The way kids use technology is constantly evolving. While these digital interactions offer convenience and engagement, they also highlight the need for parental awareness and guidance to ensure safe and responsible online behavior.

Common Online Platforms and Their Risks (Social Media, Gaming, Messaging Apps)

Social Media Platforms

Social media sites are designed for communication, entertainment, and networking. However, many platforms have minimum age requirements that are often ignored, exposing younger users to risks.

- **Instagram & Snapchat** – Popular among teens for sharing pictures and videos, but often used for private messaging. Risks include cyberbullying, exposure to inappropriate content, and privacy concerns.

- **TikTok** – Known for short videos, TikTok is widely used by children. The algorithm can expose young users to harmful trends or inappropriate videos.
- **YouTube** – While educational and entertaining, YouTube also contains unfiltered content. Kids may stumble upon misleading information or disturbing videos if parental controls aren't activated.

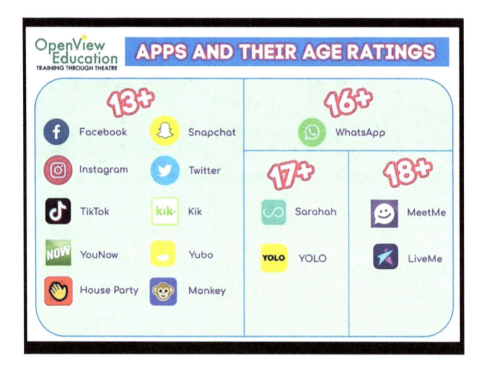

Gaming Platforms

- **Roblox & Minecraft** – These allow children to create and interact in virtual worlds, but public chat features can expose them to inappropriate interactions.

- **Fortnite & Call of Duty** – Multiplayer games with chat options that may expose kids to toxic behavior, online predators, or scams.
- **Discord** – A popular communication app for gamers that enables group chats. While useful for teamwork, it can also expose children to unmoderated conversations and strangers.

Messaging Apps

- **WhatsApp & Telegram** – Encrypted messaging apps that allow private conversations. If not monitored, kids may engage in risky conversations with unknown contacts.
- **Messenger Kids** – A safer alternative designed for children with parental controls, but it still requires supervision.

Understanding these platforms and their risks allows parents to take proactive steps in setting up safety measures and guiding their children toward healthy online interactions.

The Psychological Impact of Digital Exposure on Children

Excessive screen time and digital interactions have both positive and negative effects on a child's mental health and overall well-being. While technology can be educational and socially enriching, it can also lead to anxiety, depression, and unhealthy behavior patterns.

Positive Effects

- **Increased Connectivity** – Children can stay connected with friends and family regardless of location.

- **Educational Benefits** – Access to online learning resources enhances knowledge and skill development.
- **Creativity & Self-Expression** – Platforms like TikTok, YouTube, and gaming communities allow kids to showcase their talents and engage in creative activities.

Negative Effects

- **Social Media Comparison** – Seeing highly curated and filtered images on social media can lead to low self-esteem and body image issues.
- **Cyberbullying & Online Harassment** – Negative interactions online can cause emotional distress and mental health challenges.

Addiction & Overstimulation – The instant gratification from social media, gaming, and video content can lead to addictive behaviors, making it difficult for children to focus on offline activities.

Reduced Attention Span – Constant exposure to fast-paced digital content can make it harder for kids to focus on schoolwork and real-life conversations.

As digital exposure continues to grow, it is essential for parents to help children establish healthy habits, encourage balanced screen time, and educate them about responsible technology use.

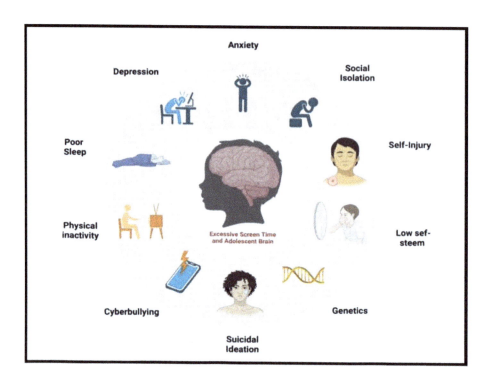

Effects of excessive screentime

Chapter 2: Cyber Threats Every Parent Should Know

The internet offers incredible opportunities for learning, entertainment, and connection. However, it also presents significant dangers, especially for children who may not yet understand the risks. As a parent, your role is to guide your child through the digital world, teaching them how to recognize and avoid online threats. This chapter will explore some of the most pressing cyber threats that children face and provide practical steps to keep them safe.

Cyberbullying: What It Is and How It Happens

Understanding Cyberbullying

Cyberbullying is the use of digital platforms to harass, humiliate, or threaten someone. Unlike traditional bullying, which happens in person, cyberbullying can occur anywhere and at any time, making it difficult for victims to escape. It often happens on social media, messaging apps, online forums, and even gaming platforms.

Common Forms of Cyberbullying

- **Harassment:** Repeatedly sending hurtful messages or threats.

- **Doxxing:** Sharing personal information online to humiliate or endanger someone.
- **Impersonation:** Creating fake accounts to spread rumors or post embarrassing content.
- **Exclusion:** Intentionally leaving someone out of online groups or conversations.
- **Outing:** Publicly revealing private or embarrassing information.

How Cyberbullying Happens

Children can be cyberbullied by classmates, strangers, or even former friends. It may start as a joke but can quickly escalate into severe emotional distress. Cyberbullying spreads quickly because digital messages, images, or videos can be forwarded to a large audience in seconds.

Steps to Protect Your Child

- **Encourage open communication.** Let your child know they can come to you if they feel uncomfortable online.
- **Monitor online activity.** Use parental controls to keep an eye on their interactions.
- **Teach them not to engage.** Responding to bullies often escalates the situation.
- **Report and block.** Most platforms allow users to report abusive content and block offenders.
- **Document incidents.** Keep screenshots of any harmful messages in case further action is needed.

Online Predators: How They Target Kids

Understanding Online Predators

Online predators are individuals who use the internet to exploit or manipulate children. They often disguise their true identity and intentions, pretending to be someone the child can trust.

How Predators Lure Children

- **Grooming:** A process where predators gradually build trust through kind words, gifts, or shared interests.
- **Fake Profiles:** Predators may pretend to be another child to befriend victims.

- **Manipulation:** Using flattery, threats, or emotional blackmail to control a child.
- **Secretive Communication:** Convincing children to hide their conversations from parents.

Warning Signs

- A child becomes secretive about online activities.
- They receive gifts from an unknown source.
- A sudden change in mood or behavior.
- Using private chat rooms or apps without parental knowledge.

Steps to Keep Your Child Safe

- **Educate them on online strangers.** Teach them that not everyone is who they claim to be.
- **Monitor friend requests.** Encourage them to only accept requests from people they know.
- **Enable privacy settings.** Ensure their accounts are private and location tracking is off.
- **Check gaming and chat apps.** Some platforms have messaging features that predators exploit.
- **Teach them to report suspicious behavior.** If anything feels off, they should tell you immediately.

Privacy Risks: The Dangers of Oversharing

What is Oversharing?

Oversharing happens when children reveal too much personal information online. This could be as simple as posting their full name, school, location, or even vacation plans. Once something is shared online, it can be difficult to take back.

Risks of Oversharing

- **Identity Theft:** Criminals can steal personal information to impersonate your child.
- **Cyberstalking:** Strangers may track a child's movements based on shared posts.
- **Exploitation:** Predators can use personal details to manipulate children.
- **Reputation Damage:** Embarrassing posts can resurface later in life.

Steps to Protect Your Child

- **Set social media accounts to private.** Only approved friends should see their posts.
- **Teach them to think before posting.** Ask, "Would I be okay with everyone seeing this?"
- **Avoid sharing location.** Turn off geotagging on photos and social media.
- **Review their friends list.** Remove anyone they don't personally know.
- **Explain that the internet is permanent.** Even deleted posts can be saved or screenshotted.

Inappropriate Content: Exposure to Violence, Hate Speech, and Adult Content

What is Inappropriate Content?

Inappropriate content includes images, videos, or discussions that are violent, sexually explicit, or filled with hate speech. Exposure to such content can negatively impact a child's emotional and psychological well-being.

Where Children Encounter Inappropriate Content

- **YouTube & Streaming Services:** Unfiltered videos may appear in recommendations.
- **Social Media:** Graphic content can be shared in posts or comments.
- **Online Games:** Some multiplayer games contain offensive language or themes.
- **Web Searches:** Innocent searches can lead to harmful sites.

How to Prevent Exposure

- **Enable parental controls.** Use Safe Search settings on browsers and YouTube Kids.
- **Use kid-friendly platforms.** Encourage platforms designed for children.
- **Teach critical thinking.** If something feels inappropriate, they should stop watching.
- **Monitor their digital habits.** Know what they are watching, playing, and reading.
- **Talk about difficult topics.** If they encounter something upsetting, discuss it calmly.

Scams and Phishing Attacks on Kids

Understanding Online Scams

Scammers often target children because they are more trusting and may not recognize fraudulent messages or fake websites. Scams can trick them into revealing personal details or even stealing money through gaming platforms.

Common Scams Targeting Kids

- **Fake Giveaways:** "Win a free gaming console! Just enter your email!"
- **Phishing Emails:** Emails pretending to be from a game or service asking for login details.
- **Fake Friend Requests:** Strangers pretending to be kids to gain access to private information.
- **In-Game Scams:** Fraudulent offers for free skins, weapons, or upgrades in online games.

Steps to Prevent Scams

- **Teach them not to click on random links.** If they get an email or message offering something free, it's likely fake.
- **Use strong passwords.** Ensure their gaming and social media accounts are protected.
- **Enable two-factor authentication.** This adds an extra layer of security.
- **Verify before sharing information.** If asked for personal details, they should check with you first.
- **Warn about too-good-to-be-true offers.** If an offer seems unrealistic, it's probably a scam.

Final Thoughts

The online world is filled with both opportunities and risks. As a parent, your best tool is **communication**. Keeping an open dialogue with your child about these dangers, setting clear rules, and using the right tools will help them navigate the internet safely. By staying involved and proactive, you can ensure that your child enjoys the benefits of the digital world while avoiding its threats.

Part 2: Monitoring & Supervising Your Child's Digital Life

Chapter 3: Setting Digital Boundaries for Kids

The internet is a vast and powerful tool, offering both education and entertainment. However, for children, unregulated internet use can lead to unhealthy habits, exposure to inappropriate content, and even online dangers. As a parent, setting clear and firm digital boundaries is crucial in ensuring your child's online experience remains safe, productive, and balanced.

This chapter will guide you through the essential steps of establishing digital rules for your child. You will learn how to determine age-appropriate internet use, create a family digital agreement, set effective screen time limits, and encourage a balance between online and offline activities. By implementing these strategies, you can foster a safe and structured digital environment for your child while teaching them responsible internet habits.

Understanding Age-Appropriate Internet Use

The internet is not a one-size-fits-all environment—what is suitable for a teenager may not be appropriate for a younger child. Understanding how children of different age groups interact with digital devices and online platforms is the first step in setting appropriate boundaries.

Why Age Matters in Digital Consumption

Children's cognitive abilities, emotional maturity, and online understanding develop at different rates. Younger children may struggle to differentiate between safe and unsafe content, while older kids may face peer pressure on social media or experience cyberbullying. Establishing age-appropriate rules ensures your child's digital exposure is beneficial rather than harmful.

Recommended Internet Use by Age

Ages 2-5:

- Minimal screen time (ideally no more than one hour per day, focusing on educational content).
- Parental supervision at all times.
- Use only child-friendly apps with strong safety controls.

Ages 6-9:

- Introduce basic internet use with strict parental guidance.
- Allow access to pre-approved educational websites and age-appropriate games.
- No social media accounts.

Ages 10-12:

- Limited supervised access to social media platforms (if allowed by parents).
- More freedom to explore the internet but with restrictions on certain content.
- Encouragement of critical thinking about online interactions.

Ages 13-18:

- More independent internet use but with clear rules on online behavior.
- Open discussions about social media risks, privacy, and cyberbullying.
- Active monitoring but respecting growing independence.

Creating a Family Digital Agreement

Once you understand age-appropriate digital use, the next step is to establish clear expectations for how technology is used in your household. A **Family Digital Agreement** is a written document that outlines the rules for internet usage, device time, and online behavior for all family members.

Why a Family Digital Agreement is Important

Having a structured set of rules makes it easier for children to understand what is expected of them. It also provides consistency and helps avoid conflicts about screen time and internet use. More importantly, it allows children to feel involved in decision-making, making them more likely to follow the rules.

Steps to Creating a Family Digital Agreement

- **Gather the Family Together:** Explain why internet safety is important and discuss concerns or challenges.
- **List the Rules:** Include guidelines such as screen time limits, acceptable websites and apps, and rules for social media use.
- **Define Consequences:** Clearly state what happens if a rule is broken (e.g., reduced screen time, loss of device privileges).
- **Agree on Responsibilities:** Parents should also commit to being good role models in digital use.
- **Write and Sign the Agreement:** Print out the rules and have every family member sign it.
- **Review Regularly:** Technology evolves, and so should your agreement. Revisit the rules periodically to ensure they remain relevant.

Establishing Screen Time Limits That Work

Children often struggle with self-regulation when it comes to screen time. Without boundaries, excessive screen time can lead to problems like poor sleep, lack of physical activity, and reduced social interactions. Setting clear and realistic screen time limits ensures that digital usage remains beneficial rather than harmful.

The Negative Effects of Unregulated Screen Time

- **Health Issues:** Too much screen time can lead to obesity, eye strain, and sleep disturbances.

- **Reduced Academic Performance:** Excessive gaming or social media use can distract from homework and studying.
- **Behavioral Changes:** Increased screen exposure can lead to irritability, addiction, and lack of focus.

How to Set Effective Screen Time Limits

- **Establish Daily Time Limits:** Follow recommended guidelines (e.g., no more than 1-2 hours for young kids, 2-3 hours for teens).
- **Schedule Screen-Free Times:** Set specific hours where no devices are allowed, such as during meals and before bedtime.
- **Encourage Alternative Activities:** Offer engaging offline activities like reading, sports, or family board games.
- **Use Parental Controls:** Enable screen time settings on devices to automatically limit usage.
- **Be Consistent:** Enforce the rules consistently to help children develop healthy habits.

Encouraging a Healthy Online-Offline Balance

Technology is a valuable tool, but it should not replace real-life experiences. Encouraging a balance between online and offline activities ensures your child develops social skills, physical health, and mental well-being.

The Importance of Offline Activities

A child who is constantly engaged in digital activities may struggle with face-to-face interactions, creativity, and outdoor play. A balanced approach allows kids to enjoy the benefits of technology without becoming overly dependent on it.

Tips to Foster a Balanced Digital Life

Set 'Device-Free' Zones: Designate areas in your home where electronic devices are not allowed, such as bedrooms and the dining table.

- **Promote Outdoor Play:** Encourage sports, bike rides, or simple outdoor activities to counteract screen time.
- **Engage in Family Activities:** Plan board game nights, cooking sessions, or creative arts to keep children engaged offline.
- **Encourage Social Interactions:** Organize playdates, family outings, or community involvement to develop interpersonal skills.
- **Be a Role Model:** If parents constantly use their phones, children will follow suit. Lead by example by balancing your own screen time.

Conclusion

Setting digital boundaries for kids is an ongoing process that requires communication, consistency, and adaptability. By understanding age-appropriate internet use, establishing a Family Digital Agreement, enforcing reasonable screen time limits, and promoting offline activities, you can help your child develop a healthy and responsible relationship with technology.

As technology continues to evolve, so should your parenting strategies. Keep an open dialogue with your child, stay informed about new digital trends, and adjust the rules as needed to maintain a safe and positive online environment for your family.

Chapter 4: Parental Controls & Monitoring Tools

As a parent in the digital age, one of the most effective ways to protect your child online is by using parental controls and monitoring tools. These tools help regulate screen time, filter inappropriate content, and track online activity, ensuring that children have a safe and positive experience on the internet. However, setting up these controls and monitoring your child's online behavior should be done thoughtfully, ensuring a balance between protection and trust.

In this chapter, we will cover the following essential topics:

- How to set up parental controls on different devices and apps.
- How to use built-in safety features available on platforms like YouTube, Google, iOS, and Android.
- A comparison of monitoring apps, including their benefits and limitations.
- Best practices for tracking online activity without violating your child's trust.

By understanding and applying these tools correctly, you can create a digital environment that encourages safety, responsibility, and open communication between you and your child.

Setting Up Parental Controls on Devices and Apps

Parental controls are software settings that allow parents to restrict and monitor their child's digital activities. These controls can help in various ways, including:

- Blocking access to inappropriate websites and content.
- Setting screen time limits to prevent excessive usage.
- Restricting purchases and downloads without parental approval.
- Monitoring messages and social media interactions.

The setup process varies depending on the device or application being used. Below are the steps to enable parental controls on common platforms.

Setting Up Parental Controls on Smartphones (iOS & Android)

For iPhones & iPads (iOS)

Apple provides built-in parental controls under the **Screen Time** settings. Follow these steps to enable them:

- Open **Settings** and tap **Screen Time**.
- Select **Turn On Screen Time** and choose whether the device belongs to a child.
- Tap **Content & Privacy Restrictions** and turn it on.
- Under **Content Restrictions**, set limits for apps, websites, and purchases.
- Use **Downtime** to schedule screen-free periods.
- Set **Communication Limits** to restrict who can contact your child via calls, messages, and FaceTime.

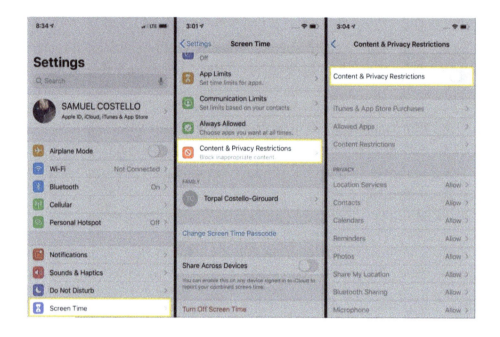

For Android Devices

Google's **Family Link** is a free app that allows parents to manage their child's device remotely. To set it up:

- Download **Google Family Link** from the Play Store.
- Open the app and follow the instructions to link your child's Google account.
- Set daily screen time limits and bedtime schedules.
- Enable SafeSearch to filter explicit content.
- Restrict app downloads and in-app purchases.
- Track device location and receive activity reports.

Parental Controls on Gaming Consoles

PlayStation

- Go to **Settings** > **Family and Parental Controls**.
- Select **Family Management** and create a child account.
- Set restrictions for communication, spending, and age-appropriate content.
- Enable playtime limits to prevent excessive gaming.

Xbox

- Visit **Settings** > **Account** > **Family Settings**.
- Add your child's account and set screen time restrictions.
- Use **Content Filters** to block inappropriate games and apps.
- Enable **Privacy & Online Safety Settings** to restrict who can communicate with your child.

How to Use Built-in Safety Features (YouTube, Google, iOS, Android)

Many digital platforms offer built-in safety features to help parents manage what their children can access. These features are often free and easy to enable.

YouTube Parental Controls

YouTube offers a **Restricted Mode** to filter inappropriate content and **YouTube Kids**, a safer version of the platform for younger users.

To Enable Restricted Mode on YouTube:

- Open **YouTube** and sign in.
- Click on your profile picture and select **Settings**.
- Scroll down and toggle on **Restricted Mode**.

YouTube Kids:

Available as a separate app, **YouTube Kids** provides curated content and parental controls for a safer viewing experience.

Google SafeSearch

Google's **SafeSearch** filters explicit content from search results.

To Enable SafeSearch:

- Go to **Google Search Settings**.
- Scroll down to **SafeSearch Filters** and toggle it on.
- **iOS and Android Safety Features**

Both iOS and Android provide options to filter content, limit downloads, and control app permissions.

iOS: Under **Settings > Screen Time > Content Restrictions**, you can block explicit content, restrict app downloads, and limit communication.

Android: Using **Google Play Parental Controls**, you can block mature content and restrict app purchases.

Monitoring Apps: The Pros and Cons

Monitoring apps offer parents additional tools to supervise their child's online activity. However, they come with both benefits and drawbacks.

Pros of Monitoring Apps

- **Real-time tracking:** Allows parents to see online activity in real-time.
- **Content filtering:** Blocks harmful content before it reaches the child.
- **Location tracking:** Helps ensure a child's physical safety.
- **Social media monitoring:** Detects cyberbullying and inappropriate conversations.

Cons of Monitoring Apps

- **Privacy concerns:** Constant tracking may make a child feel distrusted.
- **Over-reliance on technology:** Parental supervision should complement, not replace, open discussions.
- **Potential for circumvention:** Tech-savvy kids may find ways to bypass monitoring.

Popular apps like **Bark, Net Nanny, Qustodio,** and **Family Link** offer different levels of monitoring and parental control. Choosing the right one depends on your family's needs.

Tracking Online Activity Without Violating Trust

While it's essential to keep children safe, excessive monitoring can make them feel spied on. Here's how to maintain transparency while ensuring their safety:

- **Have Open Conversations** – Let your child know why monitoring is in place and how it helps them.
- **Use Parental Controls Judiciously** – Focus on safety rather than controlling every aspect of their online life.

- **Encourage Self-Regulation** – Teach kids responsible internet habits instead of relying solely on monitoring tools.
- **Review Reports Together** – Instead of secretly checking activity logs, discuss them openly to build trust.

Conclusion

Parental controls and monitoring tools are valuable resources for ensuring online safety, but they should be used thoughtfully. Setting up restrictions on devices, using built-in safety features, and finding the right balance between supervision and trust are key steps in digital parenting. By implementing these strategies, you can create a secure online environment while fostering a healthy relationship with your child in the digital world.

Chapter 5: Safe Social Media and Messaging Practices

Popular Social Media Platforms (Instagram, Snapchat, TikTok, Discord)

Social media plays a huge role in the lives of children and teenagers today. While these platforms allow kids to connect, learn, and express themselves, they also come with risks. As a parent, understanding the platforms your child uses is the first step toward keeping them safe.

Instagram

Instagram is a photo and video-sharing app that allows users to post content, follow others, and interact through likes, comments, and direct messages. While Instagram has privacy settings, children can still be exposed to inappropriate content, cyberbullying, and potential predators.

Key Risks on Instagram:

- Exposure to inappropriate content through the Explore page and Reels.
- Interaction with strangers via direct messages (DMs) and public comments.
- Pressure to gain likes and followers, leading to low self-esteem.

49

Snapchat

Snapchat is a messaging app where messages, photos, and videos disappear after being viewed. The platform's "Snap Map" feature shares a user's location, and the Stories function allows users to post content visible for 24 hours.

Key Risks on Snapchat:

- Disappearing messages can make bullying and inappropriate content harder to monitor.
- Snap Map can expose a child's location to strangers.
- Screenshots can be taken of "disappearing" content, making it permanent.

TikTok

TikTok is a short-video platform where users create and share videos with effects, music, and filters. The app has a "For You" page that recommends content based on algorithms.

Key Risks on TikTok:

- Exposure to inappropriate or harmful trends.
- Predators and scammers targeting young users through comments and messages.
- Pressure to gain followers, leading to risky behavior for social validation.

Discord

Discord is a communication app originally designed for gamers, featuring group chats (servers) and direct messaging. While it can be a great place for community engagement, it also presents risks.

Key Risks on Discord:

- Servers can have unmoderated content, exposing kids to harmful discussions.
- Strangers can add children to private servers.
- Voice chat can lead to unfiltered interactions with unknown individuals.

Setting Privacy Settings and Restrictions

Privacy settings are essential to protect your child's online identity and data. Each platform provides different options for controlling who can view a child's profile, send messages, or interact with their content. Teaching children how to manage these settings is crucial.

Steps to Enhance Privacy on Social Media

Set Accounts to Private

- On Instagram, TikTok, and Snapchat, switch the account to private so only approved followers can see posts.
- On Discord, adjust server and direct messaging settings to limit interactions with strangers.

Restrict Who Can Message Them

- Enable settings that block messages from unknown users.
- On Snapchat, only allow friends to send messages.
- On Discord, disable direct messages from non-friends.

Turn Off Location Services

- On Snapchat, disable Snap Map or set it to "Only Me."
- On Instagram, avoid posting location details.

Limit Who Can Comment or Interact

- Use Instagram's restricted mode to filter harmful comments.
- On TikTok, limit comments and duets to friends only.

Enable Parental Controls

- Use TikTok's Family Pairing to control usage.
- Set screen time limits on devices.

Teaching Kids to Recognize Fake Accounts and Scams

Fake accounts and scams are common on social media, targeting kids through fake giveaways, phishing attempts, and impersonation. Teaching children how to spot and avoid them is crucial.

Signs of Fake Accounts

- **No Profile Picture or Strange Username** – Scammers often use default avatars or random combinations of letters.
- **Few or No Followers** – Genuine accounts usually have some activity, whereas fake ones may have no posts.
- **Messages Asking for Personal Information** – Scammers may claim to offer prizes but ask for personal details.
- **Links to Unknown Websites** – Clicking on suspicious links can lead to malware or phishing scams.

How to Avoid Scams

- **Never Share Personal Information** – Kids should never give out passwords, addresses, or phone numbers.
- **Ignore and Report Suspicious Accounts** – If an account seems fake, report and block it.
- **Avoid Clicking on Unknown Links** – Phishing links often lead to fake login pages.
- **Verify Before Accepting Friend Requests** – If a child doesn't recognize someone, they shouldn't accept the request.

How to Spot and Prevent Cyberbullying

Cyberbullying is a serious issue, with children facing harassment, threats, and embarrassment online. It can happen through social media, messaging apps, and gaming platforms.

Signs of Cyberbullying

- **Sudden Change in Mood** – A child may become withdrawn or anxious after using their device.
- **Avoiding Social Media** – If a child suddenly stops using an app, they may be experiencing bullying.
- **Secretive Behavior** – Hiding their screen or avoiding conversations about online activities.
- **Upset After Reading Messages** – A child who looks distressed after using their phone may be receiving hurtful messages.

Preventing Cyberbullying

- **Encourage Open Communication** – Let children know they can talk to you about any online problems.
- **Teach Them Not to Respond** – Bullies want a reaction. Ignoring and blocking them is the best approach.
- **Report and Block Bullies** – Social media platforms have features to report abusive users.
- **Monitor Their Online Activity** – Use parental controls or check in regularly to ensure they are safe.
- **Encourage Positive Online Behavior** – Teach kids to be respectful and responsible digital citizens.

What to Do if Your Child Is Being Cyberbullied

- **Save Evidence** – Take screenshots of bullying messages.
- **Report It** – Use the platform's reporting feature.
- **Talk to Your Child** – Let them know they are not alone and that the issue can be addressed.
- **Seek Help if Necessary** – If the bullying is severe, involve teachers or counselors.

By understanding social media risks, setting privacy controls, teaching kids about scams, and addressing cyberbullying, parents can create a safer online environment. Social media is a powerful tool, but with the right guidance, children can use it responsibly while staying protected from potential dangers.

Part 3: Educating and Empowering Your Child

Chapter 6: Teaching Kids About Online Safety

The Right Way to Talk About Internet Dangers

Talking to children about internet dangers is one of the most important responsibilities of digital parenting. However, the approach matters. If the conversation is too strict or fear-based, children may become anxious or rebellious. If it is too relaxed, they may not take online threats seriously. Striking the right balance is key to ensuring that children are aware, cautious, and empowered to navigate the digital world safely.

Teach Your Kids About

- ✓ The dangers of the internet
- ✓ How to protect your identity
- ✓ Creating strong passwords
- ✓ Not engaging with strangers in person or online
- ✓ Keeping social media accounts private
- ✓ Being careful about what they post

1. Create a Safe and Open Environment

Children should feel comfortable discussing their online experiences, including any concerns or uncomfortable situations they encounter. A good way to achieve this is by fostering open communication. Instead of interrogating or making them feel guilty about their online habits, show genuine interest in their digital activities. Ask them about their favorite apps, games, and websites. This approach makes children more willing to listen when you introduce online safety topics.

2. Use Age-Appropriate Explanations

Different age groups require different levels of explanation. Younger children need simple, clear rules, while older kids and teenagers can handle more detailed discussions about risks and consequences. For example:

- **For ages 5-7:** "Some people online might pretend to be someone they're not. If anyone asks for your name or where you live, always say no and tell me."
- **For ages 8-12:** "Not everything on the internet is true. Some people spread false information, and some may try to trick you into sharing personal details. Always check with me before sharing anything."
- **For ages 13 and up:** "You have more freedom online, but that also comes with responsibility. Be mindful of what you share, who you interact with, and the information you trust."

3. Focus on Positive and Practical Solutions

Instead of only warning about dangers, emphasize what they *should* do to stay safe. Teach them how to use privacy settings, report suspicious behavior, and verify sources of information. Providing solutions alongside warnings makes children feel more in control rather than fearful.

4. Encourage Questions and Discussions

Let your child ask questions about anything they don't understand. If they bring up scenarios from their online experiences, take the opportunity to discuss what was safe and what could have been handled differently. If you don't know the answer to something, research it together.

Teaching Kids to Identify and Handle Cyberbullying

Cyberbullying is one of the most common online dangers for children and teenagers. It can happen through social media, messaging apps, online games, or even school forums. The effects of cyberbullying can be serious, leading to anxiety, depression, and low self-esteem. Teaching kids how to recognize and respond to cyberbullying is essential.

1. Explain What Cyberbullying Looks Like

Many children may not immediately recognize cyberbullying, especially if it starts subtly. Describe the different forms cyberbullying can take:

- **Harassment:** Repeated mean messages, threats, or name-calling.
- **Spreading rumors:** False information shared to harm someone's reputation.
- **Exclusion:** Purposely leaving someone out of group chats or online activities.
- **Impersonation:** Someone pretending to be them or another person to cause harm.
- **Public shaming:** Posting embarrassing photos or videos without permission.

2. Teach the "Stop, Block, and Tell" Strategy

Children need a clear plan for handling cyberbullying when it occurs. A simple method is:

- **Stop:** Do not reply or engage with the bully.

- **Block:** Use built-in blocking tools on apps and websites to prevent further contact.
- **Tell:** Inform a trusted adult, whether a parent, teacher, or counselor.

3. Reinforce the Importance of Kindness and Empathy

Children should understand that their own online behavior matters. Teach them to be kind, avoid spreading rumors, and stand up for others who are being bullied. Encourage them to report bullying if they see it happening to a friend.

How to Talk About Online Predators Without Scaring Them

The topic of online predators is particularly sensitive. While children need to understand the risks, scaring them too much may cause unnecessary fear or secrecy. The goal is to educate them in a way that makes them feel empowered rather than helpless.

1. Explain the Concept of Online Strangers

Young children understand "stranger danger" in real life, but they may not see online strangers as a risk. Explain that, just like in the real world, not everyone online is trustworthy. Some people pretend to be kids to trick others.

2. Teach the Signs of a Suspicious Person Online

Predators often try to gain trust before asking for personal information or inappropriate things. Teach your child to watch out for these red flags:

- Someone who asks them to keep their conversations a secret.
- Someone who wants personal details like their age, school, or home address.
- Someone who tries to send them gifts or money.
- Someone who wants to move conversations to private platforms like text messaging or video calls.

3. Set Clear Rules About Online Communication

- Make sure your child knows the family rules about talking to strangers online:
- Never share personal information, even if the person seems friendly.
- Avoid private chats with people they don't know in real life.
- Always ask a parent before adding a new online friend.
- If something feels off, trust their instincts and tell an adult.

Encouraging Critical Thinking About Online Content

The internet is filled with a mix of useful information, misleading content, and outright falsehoods. Teaching children how to think critically about what they see online is one of the best ways to protect them from misinformation, scams, and manipulation.

1. Teach Them to Question Everything

Encourage kids to ask themselves:

- **Who posted this?** Is the source credible?

- **Why was this posted?** Is it meant to inform, entertain, or manipulate?
- **Is there evidence?** Are there reliable sources backing up the claim?
- **Does it seem too good to be true?** If so, it probably is.

2. Show Them How to Verify Information

Instead of just telling kids not to trust everything online, show them how to check:

- Use fact-checking websites like Snopes or Google Fact Check.
- Cross-check news stories on multiple trusted websites.
- Look for the original source of viral posts and videos.

3. Explain the Impact of Misinformation

Discuss real-life examples of fake news or hoaxes and how they influenced people. Help them understand that false information can spread quickly and cause harm.

4. Encourage Healthy Skepticism

A good rule for kids is: *If you're unsure about something online, ask a parent or teacher before believing or sharing it.*

By following these steps, parents can ensure that their children are well-informed, cautious, and confident in navigating the digital world safely. With the right guidance, kids can enjoy the benefits of technology while staying protected from its dangers.

Chapter 7: Digital Footprint & Online Reputation

What Is a Digital Footprint?

Every time your child goes online, they leave behind a trail of information known as a **digital footprint**. This footprint consists of everything they do on the internet—social media posts, comments, likes, shared photos, online searches, and even the websites they visit.

A digital footprint can be **active** or **passive**:

- **Active Digital Footprint**: This is the information a person knowingly shares, such as posting on social media, commenting on videos, or uploading pictures.
- **Passive Digital Footprint**: This is data collected about a person without them actively providing it, such as websites tracking browsing history or apps collecting location data.

Unlike footprints in the sand that wash away, **a digital footprint is often permanent**. Even if a child deletes a post or account, copies or screenshots might still exist elsewhere. This makes it crucial to **teach kids the importance of managing their online presence responsibly**.

How Kids' Online Actions Affect Their Future

Many children and teenagers do not realize that their online activity today could impact their **education, career opportunities, and personal life** in the future. Colleges, employers, and even sports teams often check an applicant's online presence before making decisions. Here's how a child's digital footprint can shape their future:

1. College Admissions

Many universities review applicants' social media profiles to get a sense of their character. **Inappropriate posts, offensive language, or negative behavior** online could hurt a student's chances of admission.

2. Job Opportunities

Even as teenagers, kids should be mindful of what they post online. **Potential employers often check social media** before hiring. A single careless post could lead to lost opportunities in the future.

3. Reputation Among Peers and Community

A poor online reputation can **damage relationships** with friends, family, teachers, and mentors. If a child shares something harmful or embarrassing, it can spread quickly and lead to social consequences, including bullying or exclusion.

4. Legal and Safety Risks

Certain online activities, like **cyberbullying, harassment, or sharing inappropriate content**, could have legal consequences. Schools and authorities take these matters seriously, and actions taken online can sometimes result in real-world punishments.

To protect their future, children must learn that **what they do online today stays with them for years to come**. It's essential to build a positive digital footprint instead of one that might harm their future goals.

The Risks of Posting Personal Information

Many children share personal details online without understanding the potential dangers. While it may seem harmless to post a photo or update a status, certain information can be misused in ways they might not expect. Here are the major risks of **sharing personal details online**:

1. Identity Theft

Even small pieces of personal information—such as a **full name, birthday, school name, or address**—can be used by cybercriminals to steal identities. Scammers may try to impersonate children or gain access to sensitive accounts.

2. Stranger Danger & Online Predators

Children who share too much personal information may **unintentionally attract strangers**. A child revealing their **school name, daily routine, or favorite hangout spots** might give predators the information they need to approach them in real life.

3. Cyberbullying & Harassment

If a child shares **embarrassing pictures, controversial opinions, or private thoughts** online, others may use this information to **harass**

or bully them. Even something harmless can be twisted or used against them later.

4. Unwanted Digital Trail

Once something is posted online, it's often impossible to **completely erase it**. Even if the original post is deleted, someone may have taken a **screenshot or saved a copy**. Kids must understand that what they share today could resurface in the future.

To stay safe, children should follow these golden rules:

- **Never share personal details** like home addresses, phone numbers, or school names publicly.
- **Be cautious about sharing photos**, especially ones that reveal locations or personal habits.
- **Think before sharing opinions or sensitive information**, as words can be taken out of context and resurface later.

Teaching Kids to Think Before They Share

The best way to protect a child's digital footprint is by teaching them the habit of **thinking critically before posting anything online**. Here are some simple **guidelines for kids to follow** before sharing:

1. Pause Before Posting

Encourage kids to ask themselves:

- **Would I be okay if my teacher, parent, or future employer saw this?**
- **Am I comfortable with this post being online forever?**

- **Could this post hurt someone's feelings or cause trouble?**

2. Use the T.H.I.N.K. Rule

Teach kids to use the **T.H.I.N.K. test** before posting:

> **T** - Is it **True**?
>
> **H** - Is it **Helpful**?
>
> **I** - Is it **Inspiring**?
>
> **N** - Is it **Necessary**?
>
> **K** - Is it **Kind**?

If the post fails any of these, it's better **not to share it**.

3. Understand Privacy Settings

Help kids set their social media accounts to **private** so that only trusted people can see their posts. Teach them how to **block, report, or mute** anyone who makes them uncomfortable.

4. Avoid Sharing Location Information

Many apps **automatically track and share locations**. Teach kids to turn off location sharing on social media and avoid mentioning specific places in their posts.

5. Respect Others' Privacy

Teach kids that **not all moments should be shared online**. Posting **photos of friends without permission** or **spreading rumors** can damage relationships and reputations.

6. Think About the Future

Remind kids that **the internet never forgets**. Posts made in anger or frustration can have long-term consequences. Teach them that if they wouldn't say it **in person**, they shouldn't say it online.

Final Thoughts

A child's digital footprint **shapes their online reputation** and affects their future opportunities. By helping them understand what a digital footprint is, how their online actions can impact their future, and the risks of oversharing, parents can **equip their children with the knowledge to navigate the internet safely**.

The goal is not to scare kids away from the internet but to **teach them to be responsible digital citizens**. By building good online habits early, children can create a **positive digital legacy** that will benefit them for years to come.

Chapter 8: Safe Online Gaming for Kids

Gaming is an exciting and engaging activity for kids, offering entertainment, creativity, and even educational benefits. However, the online gaming world also comes with risks that every parent should be aware of. Understanding these dangers and implementing protective measures will help ensure that your child has a safe and positive gaming experience.

The Risks of Online Gaming (Chat Rooms, Microtransactions, Addiction)

1. Chat Rooms and Online Interactions

Many online games allow players to communicate with others through chat rooms, voice chat, or direct messaging. While this feature can enhance teamwork and socialization, it also exposes children to potential dangers, including:

- **Strangers with bad intentions:** Not everyone in an online game is a fellow child or a friendly gamer. Some individuals use these platforms to approach kids in deceptive ways.

- **Inappropriate language or content:** Without proper moderation, chat rooms can expose children to foul language, hate speech, or even discussions about adult topics.
- **Peer pressure and bullying:** Online interactions sometimes lead to cyberbullying, where players harass or pressure others into certain behaviors.

2. Microtransactions and In-Game Purchases

Many online games offer in-game purchases, allowing players to buy character upgrades, skins, or power-ups using real money. Kids may not fully understand the value of money, leading to unintended purchases or financial loss. Some risks include:

- **Excessive spending:** Games often use strategies to encourage frequent spending, such as limited-time offers and reward systems.
- **Accidental purchases:** Without safeguards, children might unknowingly buy expensive items linked to a parent's credit card.
- **Pay-to-win mechanics:** Some games offer advantages for those who spend money, leading kids to feel pressured to buy items to keep up with others.

3. Gaming Addiction and Screen Time Overload

Excessive gaming can interfere with a child's daily life, including school, sleep, and social activities. Signs of gaming addiction include:

- Irritability or distress when not playing
- Skipping meals or sleep to continue gaming
- Neglecting schoolwork or outdoor activities
- Constantly talking about or thinking about the game

By being aware of these risks, parents can take proactive steps to create a safe gaming environment.

Setting Boundaries for Safe Gaming

Establishing clear rules about when, where, and how long your child can play games is crucial for maintaining a balanced lifestyle. Here's how to set healthy gaming boundaries:

1. Define Screen Time Limits

Set daily or weekly time limits based on your child's age and responsibilities. The American Academy of Pediatrics recommends:

- **Ages 2-5:** No more than one hour of screen time per day.
- **Ages 6-12:** One to two hours of recreational screen time per day.
- **Teens:** Moderate use with breaks and a balance of offline activities.

Encourage your child to take breaks every 30-60 minutes to rest their eyes and engage in other activities.

2. Designate a Safe Gaming Area

Keep gaming devices in a shared family space rather than in bedrooms. This allows parents to monitor gaming behavior and ensure children are not engaging in unsafe activities online.

3. Enable Parental Controls

Most gaming consoles, apps, and online services offer parental control settings that allow parents to:

- Restrict online interactions
- Set time limits
- Block inappropriate content
- Disable in-game purchases

Take time to explore and activate these settings based on your child's age and gaming habits.

Recognizing and Avoiding In-Game Scams and Predators

Scammers and online predators target children through games, often using deceptive tactics to steal information or lure kids into unsafe situations. Here's how to teach your child to recognize and avoid them:

1. Avoid Sharing Personal Information

Teach children to never share personal details, such as their real name, school, address, or phone number, while playing online games. Predators may disguise themselves as friendly players to gain trust.

2. Be Wary of Free Items and "Too Good to Be True" Offers

Scammers often trick players by offering free in-game currency, rare items, or cheats. These scams usually involve clicking on links that lead to phishing sites, which steal login credentials or personal data.

Tip: If an offer seems too good to be true, it probably is. Encourage kids to check with a parent before accepting gifts from strangers online.

3. Report and Block Suspicious Players

If your child encounters a player making inappropriate comments or pressuring them into private chats, they should immediately:

- **Block the user** to prevent further communication.
- **Report the behavior** to the game's moderation team.
- **Inform a trusted adult** about the incident.

Encourage an open dialogue where your child feels comfortable discussing any online encounters that make them uncomfortable.

Selecting Age-Appropriate Games

Choosing the right games for your child helps reduce exposure to inappropriate content and online risks. Follow these guidelines when selecting games:

1. Check the Game's Rating

Game rating systems, such as the ESRB (Entertainment Software Rating Board), provide guidance on age-appropriate content:

- **E (Everyone):** Suitable for all ages
- **E10+ (Everyone 10 and Up):** Mild content, suitable for older children
- **T (Teen):** May contain violence, language, or suggestive themes

- **M (Mature):** Intended for ages 17+ due to explicit content

2. Read Reviews and Parent Guides

Before allowing your child to play a game, read online reviews from trusted sources, check the game's community guidelines, and see what other parents say about it.

3. Test the Game Yourself

If possible, play the game for a short period to see if the content aligns with your family's values and safety standards.

4. Prefer Games with Offline or Limited Online Interactions

Look for games that offer offline modes or controlled online interactions, such as:

- Minecraft (creative mode with parental settings)
- Super Mario Series (offline adventure games)
- LEGO games (story-based, child-friendly experiences)

Final Thoughts

Online gaming can be a fun and enriching experience when approached with caution and responsibility. By understanding the risks, setting clear rules, and choosing appropriate games, parents can help their children develop safe gaming habits that will benefit them in the long run.

Encourage open conversations with your child about their gaming experiences, and remind them that safety always comes first. With the right approach, gaming can remain an enjoyable activity without compromising security or well-being.

Part 4: Protecting Your Child from Cyber Threats

Chapter 9: Cybersecurity Basics for Families

The internet is a wonderful place for learning, communication, and entertainment. However, it also comes with risks that can affect both children and adults. As a family, understanding and practicing cybersecurity is essential to keeping your personal information safe and protecting yourself from cyber threats. This chapter will cover fundamental cybersecurity practices, including creating strong passwords, using two-factor authentication, safe browsing habits, recognizing and avoiding scams, and what to do if an account gets hacked.

Creating Strong Passwords and Using Two-Factor Authentication

Understanding the Importance of Strong Passwords

Passwords are the first line of defense against hackers. A weak password can be easily guessed, allowing cybercriminals to access your accounts, steal personal information, or even lock you out. Many people make the mistake of using simple passwords like "123456," "password," or their pet's name, making it easier for hackers to break in.

A **strong password** should:

- Be at least 12–16 characters long
- Include a mix of uppercase and lowercase letters
- Contain numbers and special characters (!, @, #, $, etc.)
- Avoid easily guessed words like birthdays, names, or common phrases

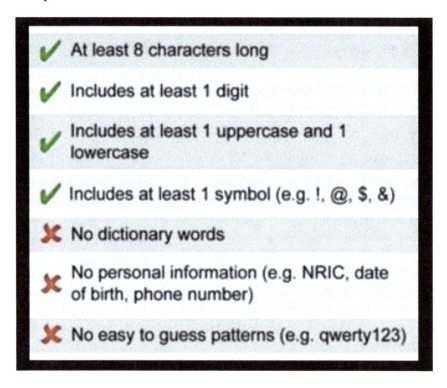

Steps to Create a Strong Password

- Think of a phrase that is meaningful to you but hard for others to guess. Example: "I love hiking in the mountains!"
- Convert it into a strong password by using abbreviations and symbols: **"1Lh!nTh3M!"**

- Avoid using the same password for multiple accounts. If one account is compromised, others can be too.
- Consider using a **password manager** to securely store and generate strong passwords.

Using Two-Factor Authentication (2FA)

Two-Factor Authentication (2FA) adds an extra layer of security by requiring a second form of verification, such as a code sent to your phone or email, in addition to your password.

How to Enable 2FA:

- Go to your account's security settings (Google, Facebook, Instagram, etc.).
- Select **Two-Factor Authentication** or **Multi-Factor Authentication**.
- Choose a method: SMS text, authentication app (Google Authenticator, Authy), or biometric verification (fingerprint, face ID).
- Follow the prompts to set it up.

By enabling 2FA, even if a hacker steals your password, they won't be able to access your account without the second verification step.

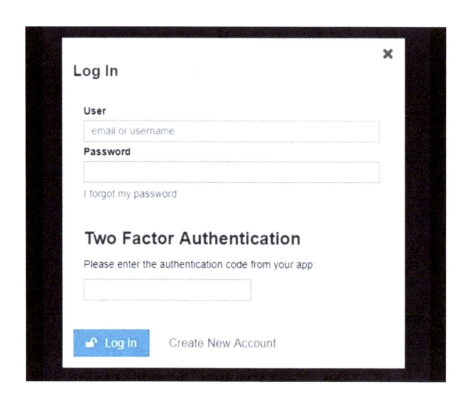

Safe Browsing Practices for Kids

The Risks of Unsupervised Browsing

The internet contains valuable educational content, but it also has harmful sites that expose children to inappropriate content, scams, and dangerous interactions with strangers. Teaching kids safe browsing habits can protect them from these risks.

Safe Browsing Tips for Kids

- **Use Kid-Friendly Browsers and Search Engines** – Set up Google SafeSearch or use kid-friendly search engines like Kiddle and KidRex.

- **Enable Parental Controls** – Most browsers and devices have parental control settings that limit access to inappropriate content.
- **Teach Kids to Recognize Secure Websites** – Safe websites have "HTTPS" in the URL and a padlock icon.
- **Avoid Clicking on Suspicious Links** – Teach kids never to click on pop-ups, ads, or random links in emails.
- **Never Share Personal Information** – Kids should never share their name, address, school, or contact details online.

Setting Up Safe Browsing Tools

- **Google SafeSearch:** Go to Google Settings > Search Settings > Turn on SafeSearch.
- **YouTube Restricted Mode:** Go to YouTube Settings > General > Enable Restricted Mode.
- **Use Family-Friendly Browsers:** Install apps like Microsoft Family Safety or Net Nanny to filter content.

Avoiding Scams and Phishing Attacks

What is Phishing?

Phishing is when scammers try to trick you into giving away personal information by pretending to be someone you trust, like a bank, social media platform, or online store. They often use fake emails, text messages, or pop-ups to steal passwords and credit card details.

How to Recognize Phishing Scams

- **Unexpected Emails or Messages** – If you receive an email claiming to be from a bank, but you never requested anything, it's likely fake.
- **Urgency or Fear Tactics** – Scammers often say, "Your account will be locked in 24 hours! Click here now!"
- **Misspellings and Bad Grammar** – Legitimate companies proofread their messages; phishing emails often contain errors.
- **Strange or Mismatched Email Addresses** – Always check if the sender's email matches the official website.

Steps to Avoid Phishing Attacks

- **Do Not Click Suspicious Links** – Hover over links to check their real destination before clicking.
- **Verify with the Source** – If you get an email from your bank, call them directly instead of clicking the link.
- **Use Security Software** – Many antivirus programs can detect phishing attempts and block them.
- **Educate Kids** – Teach children never to open messages from unknown senders.

How to Handle a Hacked Account

Signs Your Account Might Be Hacked

- You can't log in even with the correct password.
- Friends receive strange messages from you.
- Unfamiliar transactions appear in your online accounts.
- Your account settings have changed without your permission.

Steps to Take If Your Account is Hacked

- **Change Your Password Immediately** – Use a strong, new password that is completely different from the old one.
- **Enable Two-Factor Authentication (2FA)** – This adds another layer of security.
- **Log Out of All Devices** – Many platforms allow you to sign out remotely from all devices.
- **Check for Unauthorized Activity** – Review your account for any suspicious changes or logins.

- **Contact the Platform's Support Team** – Report the hack to the website or service provider.
- **Warn Friends and Family** – If your social media or email was hacked, let your contacts know not to trust messages from your account.
- **Scan Your Device for Malware** – Run a security scan to check if a virus or keylogger caused the hack.

Preventing Future Hacks

- Regularly update passwords.
- Avoid using the same password across multiple accounts.
- Use an antivirus program to detect threats early.
- Monitor your online accounts for suspicious activity.

Final Thoughts

Cybersecurity is an ongoing process that requires awareness and proactive measures. By implementing these basic cybersecurity practices, families can create a safer online environment for both children and adults. Encourage open discussions about digital safety, stay informed about emerging threats, and always prioritize online security. Keeping your family's digital world secure starts with simple, everyday habits that make a huge difference.

Chapter 10: Dealing with Cyberbullying

Understanding Cyberbullying

Cyberbullying is a form of harassment that occurs through digital platforms such as social media, messaging apps, gaming communities, and even emails. Unlike traditional bullying, cyberbullying can be relentless, reaching children anywhere and at any time. The anonymity of the internet can also embolden bullies, making online harassment more aggressive and damaging.

As a parent, recognizing and addressing cyberbullying is essential to protecting your child's emotional well-being. This chapter will guide you through identifying signs of cyberbullying, taking appropriate action, and empowering your child to handle online harassment.

How to Spot Signs Your Child is Being Cyberbullied

Many children do not openly discuss being cyberbullied due to fear, shame, or embarrassment. However, certain behavioral and emotional changes may indicate that they are experiencing online harassment. As a parent, staying observant and proactive can help you intervene early.

Emotional and Behavioral Signs

- **Sudden Mood Swings:** Your child may become withdrawn, anxious, or irritable after using their phone or computer.
- **Loss of Interest in Technology:** A child who previously enjoyed social media or online games may suddenly avoid them.
- **Reluctance to Attend School or Social Gatherings:** Cyberbullying often extends into real-life interactions, making children fearful of their peers.
- **Frequent Headaches or Stomach Aches:** Stress-related symptoms can indicate emotional distress caused by cyberbullying.
- **Low Self-Esteem:** Your child may express feelings of worthlessness, sadness, or self-doubt after being targeted online.

Behavioral Changes in Online Activity

- **Deleting or Avoiding Social Media Accounts:** Your child may suddenly deactivate or delete their profiles to escape online abuse.
- **Nervousness When Receiving Messages or Notifications:** If your child appears uneasy when receiving online messages, it could indicate harassment.
- **Blocking or Unfriending People Frequently:** A sudden increase in blocking accounts may be an attempt to escape a bully.

- **Hiding Screens from Parents:** A child who quickly minimizes their screen or hides their device may be trying to prevent you from seeing upsetting messages.

If you notice any of these signs, have an open and supportive conversation with your child. Reassure them that they are not alone and that you are there to help.

Steps to Take if Your Child is a Victim

If you confirm that your child is being cyberbullied, immediate action is necessary to ensure their safety and well-being. Follow these steps to address the situation effectively:

Step 1: Stay Calm and Listen

Your child needs to feel safe and supported. Instead of reacting with anger or panic, calmly listen to their experience. Let them explain the situation in their own words and reassure them that they are not at fault.

Step 2: Document the Bullying

Encourage your child to save all messages, screenshots, emails, and posts related to the bullying. These records will be essential when reporting the harassment to schools, platforms, or law enforcement.

Step 3: Help Them Secure Their Online Accounts

Cyberbullies often create fake accounts or use multiple platforms to harass their victims. To protect your child:

- Change passwords to all accounts.
- Enable two-factor authentication where possible.
- Adjust privacy settings to limit who can contact them.
- Block the bully on all platforms.

Step 4: Avoid Retaliation

Teach your child not to respond aggressively or engage with the bully. Responding may escalate the situation and give the bully more power. Instead, encourage them to ignore and report the harassment.

Step 5: Report and Seek Support

Cyberbullying should never be handled alone. Reach out to teachers, school counselors, online platform moderators, or law enforcement if necessary.

Teaching Kids to Respond to Online Harassment

Equipping your child with the right strategies to handle cyberbullying will empower them to navigate online spaces confidently. Here are ways to help them respond effectively:

1. Encourage Open Communication

Let your child know they can always come to you if they face any form of online harassment. Establish a safe and judgment-free space for them to share their experiences.

2. Teach the 'Ignore, Block, Report' Method

- **Ignore:** Teach them not to engage with bullies. Most online bullies seek reactions, and ignoring them can sometimes make them stop.
- **Block:** Encourage them to use the block feature on social media, messaging apps, and gaming platforms to prevent further contact.
- **Report:** Show them how to report abuse on different platforms. Reporting can lead to the bully's account being restricted or removed.

3. Practice Assertive Responses

If ignoring is not an option, teach your child how to respond assertively without being aggressive. Examples include:

- "I will not engage in negativity. Please stop."
- "I don't appreciate this behavior. It's hurtful and unnecessary."

4. Build Resilience and Confidence

Cyberbullying can take a toll on self-esteem. Encourage activities that build confidence, such as sports, hobbies, or group activities where they feel valued and supported.

When to Report Cyberbullying (to Schools, Platforms, Law Enforcement)

While some cyberbullying incidents can be handled by blocking and ignoring the bully, others require serious intervention. Here's when and how to escalate the situation:

1. Reporting to Social Media and Online Platforms

Most platforms have built-in tools to report harassment, hate speech, and bullying. Steps to report vary by platform, but generally involve:

- Navigating to the offending post or message.
- Selecting the "Report" option.
- Providing details about the harassment.

2. Reporting to Schools

If cyberbullying involves classmates or impacts your child's school life, report it to school officials. Schools often have anti-bullying policies and can take action to prevent further incidents.

3. Involving Law Enforcement

If cyberbullying includes threats of violence, stalking, identity theft, or sexual exploitation, report it to law enforcement immediately. Provide:

- Screenshots of threats or harassment.
- Details of accounts involved.
- Any relevant timeline of incidents.

Final Thoughts

Cyberbullying is a serious issue that requires awareness, communication, and action. As a parent, being proactive and informed will help you guide your child through challenges in the digital world. By recognizing the signs, taking the right steps, and teaching them to respond appropriately, you can create a safe online environment for your child.

Always remind your child that they are not alone—support is available, and cyberbullying can be stopped.

Chapter 11: Protecting Kids from Online Predators

T he internet has opened up a world of possibilities for children, providing them with entertainment, learning opportunities, and ways to connect with friends. However, it also comes with dangers—one of the most alarming being online predators. These individuals use deception, manipulation, and emotional exploitation to target children and teens, often leading to serious harm. As a parent, it is crucial to understand how online predators operate, recognize the warning signs, and take the necessary steps to protect your child from potential danger.

How Predators Lure Kids Online

Online predators are skilled manipulators who know how to exploit a child's curiosity, trust, and desire for friendship. They use various tactics to groom and manipulate children into dangerous situations. Understanding these methods will help parents stay vigilant and proactive.

1. Building Trust Through False Identities

One of the most common tactics predators use is creating fake profiles on social media, gaming platforms, or chat apps. They may pose as someone close in age to your child, such as a fellow teenager with similar interests. This false identity allows them to gain your child's trust over time.

2. Engaging in Friendly Conversations

Predators often start conversations casually, discussing topics that interest children, such as video games, TV shows, or hobbies. They aim to make the child feel comfortable and establish a sense of friendship before gradually steering the conversation toward more personal or inappropriate topics.

3. Offering Gifts, Rewards, or Attention

Children who feel lonely, insecure, or in need of validation may be drawn in by predators who offer them compliments, special attention, or even digital gifts like game credits, exclusive content, or in-game items. These seemingly innocent gestures are used to create emotional dependence.

4. Encouraging Secrets and Isolation

A major red flag is when an online acquaintance asks a child to keep their conversations secret. Predators often use secrecy as a tool to manipulate and control their victims. They may tell the child that their parents "wouldn't understand" or "would be mad," discouraging them from seeking help.

5. Manipulating Emotions and Guilt

Once a predator gains trust, they may use emotional tactics to guilt the child into compliance. They may say things like, "I thought you trusted me," or, "If you really liked me, you'd do this for me." This emotional blackmail can make children feel pressured to follow the predator's requests.

6. Requesting Personal Information or Photos

Eventually, predators may try to obtain personal details such as home addresses, phone numbers, or school names. They may also attempt to solicit inappropriate images or videos, which can lead to blackmail or exploitation.

7. Arranging In-Person Meetings

The ultimate goal for many predators is to meet the child in person. They may suggest meeting secretly at a mall, park, or another location. Some may even pretend to be in trouble, claiming they "need help" as a way to lure the child into agreeing to a meeting.

Warning Signs to Watch for in Your Child's Online Behavior

While some children may openly discuss their online activities, many do not realize when they are being groomed, or they may feel too embarrassed or scared to tell their parents. As a parent, staying alert to changes in your child's behavior can help you detect warning signs early.

1. Increased Secrecy About Online Activities

If your child suddenly becomes very private about their internet use, minimizes screens when you walk by, or refuses to share what they are doing online, it could be a sign that someone is influencing them inappropriately.

2. Receiving Gifts or Money from Unknown Sources

If your child starts receiving money, digital credits, gaming accessories, or even physical gifts without a reasonable explanation, it could be a sign of an online predator attempting to build trust.

3. Sudden Changes in Mood or Behavior

Victims of online grooming often experience mood swings, anxiety, depression, or withdrawal from family and friends. If your child appears unusually sad, nervous, or irritable, it may indicate something is wrong.

4. Talking About a 'New Friend' They Won't Share Details About

If your child frequently mentions a new friend they met online but refuses to provide details or gets defensive when questioned, this could be a cause for concern.

5. Using New Apps or Websites Without Your Knowledge

Predators often use lesser-known chat apps or gaming platforms that offer anonymity. If your child suddenly starts using new platforms without discussing them, investigate what they are accessing.

6. Speaking or Typing in Coded Language

Some children who are being manipulated may start using unusual abbreviations, symbols, or phrases that they didn't use before, possibly as a way to communicate secretly with an online predator.

7. Attempts to Sneak Out or Unexplained Absences

If your child suddenly tries to leave the house without explanation, especially at odd hours, they may be planning an in-person meeting with an online acquaintance.

Steps to Take If You Suspect Online Grooming

If you suspect your child is being groomed online, it's essential to act quickly but carefully. Taking the right steps can protect your child and prevent further harm.

1. Stay Calm and Approach Your Child with Care

Avoid immediately scolding or blaming your child, as this may make them defensive or scared. Instead, approach the conversation with concern and an open mind.

2. Review Their Online Activity

Check browser history, chat messages, and recent contacts on their devices. Look for unfamiliar names, unusual conversations, or requests from strangers.

3. Block and Report the Suspect

If you identify a suspicious individual, immediately block them on all platforms and report their profile to the platform administrators.

4. Strengthen Privacy Settings

Ensure your child's social media accounts have strict privacy settings. Enable parental controls to monitor new contacts and restrict messaging from strangers.

5. Encourage Open Communication

Make sure your child understands that they can talk to you about anything without fear of punishment. Let them know they are not in trouble, but rather, you are there to protect them.

6. Contact Authorities if Necessary

If the situation is serious, contact law enforcement or a cybercrime unit. Online grooming is illegal, and predators should be investigated.

Reporting Suspicious Activity

If you come across a potential online predator or witness suspicious behavior, reporting it is crucial in preventing harm to other children.

1. Report Directly to the Platform

Most social media sites, messaging apps, and online games have reporting tools to flag inappropriate behavior. Use these features to alert moderators.

2. Contact Local Law Enforcement

If you believe a predator is actively targeting children, report the details to your local police or cybercrime division.

3. Use Online Reporting Agencies

Organizations such as the **National Center for Missing & Exploited Children (NCMEC)** or **CyberTipline** allow you to submit anonymous tips regarding suspected child exploitation.

4. Educate Your Child About Reporting

Teach your child how to recognize red flags and report inappropriate behavior themselves. Encourage them to speak up if they ever feel uncomfortable online.

Final Thoughts

Protecting children from online predators requires vigilance, education, and open communication. By understanding how predators operate, recognizing warning signs, and taking proactive steps, parents can create a safer online environment for their children. Remember, your child's safety starts with awareness and trust—build a relationship where they feel comfortable discussing their online experiences with you.

Part 5: Advanced Strategies for Digital Parenting

Chapter 12: Raising Tech-Savvy and Responsible Digital Citizens

---

Teaching Kids Ethical Online Behavior

The internet is a powerful tool that offers endless opportunities for learning, communication, and entertainment. However, it also comes with responsibilities. Just like in the real world, children need to understand the importance of ethical behavior when interacting online. Ethical online behavior means using the internet in a way that is respectful, responsible, and safe for both themselves and others.

Understanding Online Ethics

Teaching kids about online ethics involves helping them recognize the impact of their actions in digital spaces. Many children may not realize that their words and behavior online carry consequences, just like they do in face-to-face interactions. Ethics online include:

Respecting Others – Treating people with kindness and avoiding cyberbullying or rude comments.

Protecting Privacy – Keeping personal information safe and not sharing others' details without consent.

Being Honest – Avoiding false representation, plagiarism, or spreading misinformation.

Following Rules – Respecting terms of service for websites and apps.

Thinking Before Posting – Understanding that anything shared online can be permanent and impact future opportunities.

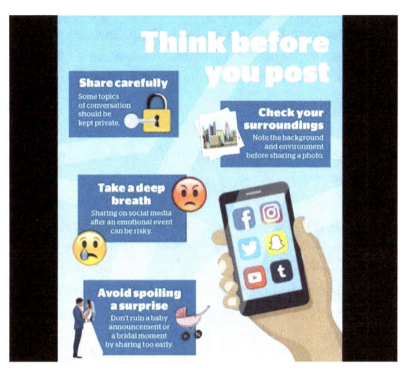

Steps to Teach Kids Ethical Online Behavior

- **Lead by Example** – Kids learn best from observing their parents and teachers. Model ethical behavior by practicing respectful communication and responsible technology use.
- **Have Open Conversations** – Discuss with children what ethical online behavior looks like and why it matters.
- **Set Digital Rules** – Establish guidelines about appropriate content, respectful interactions, and responsible sharing.
- **Encourage Empathy** – Teach kids to consider how their words and actions affect others before posting or commenting.

- **Explain Consequences** – Help them understand that inappropriate behavior online can lead to account suspensions, legal trouble, or damaged reputations.
- **Practice Good Digital Citizenship** – Encourage children to contribute positively to online communities by reporting harmful behavior and sharing helpful content.

Helping Kids Navigate Misinformation and Fake News

The internet is filled with an overwhelming amount of information, but not everything found online is true. Misinformation and fake news are major concerns, especially for children who may not yet have the critical thinking skills to distinguish between factual and misleading content. Teaching kids how to identify and verify information is crucial for developing responsible digital citizens.

Understanding Misinformation and Fake News

Misinformation refers to incorrect or misleading information spread unintentionally, while fake news is deliberately false content designed to mislead readers. Both can spread rapidly through social media, websites, and messaging apps. Common types include:

- **Clickbait Headlines** – Sensationalized or exaggerated headlines meant to grab attention.
- **Deepfakes and Manipulated Media** – Edited videos or images that misrepresent reality.
- **Satire and Parody** – Articles or posts meant to entertain but sometimes mistaken as real news.

- **Bias and Opinion Disguised as News** – Content that pushes a particular viewpoint rather than presenting factual, balanced information.

Steps to Teach Kids to Identify Misinformation

- **Encourage Critical Thinking** – Teach kids to question what they read, see, or hear online before believing or sharing it.
- **Check the Source** – Help them identify credible sources by looking for well-known, reliable news outlets and official websites.
- **Verify Information** – Show them how to cross-check facts using multiple trusted sources.
- **Look at the URL** – Some fake news websites mimic real ones but have slightly altered URLs (e.g., "newsreport.com" vs. "newsreport.net").
- **Recognize Bias** – Discuss how some articles may be written with an agenda and encourage them to seek balanced perspectives.
- **Be Wary of Emotional Manipulation** – Teach kids that fake news often plays on emotions like fear or anger to get more engagement.
- **Use Fact-Checking Websites** – Introduce them to resources like Snopes or FactCheck.org to verify questionable claims.
- **Pause Before Sharing** – Encourage kids to think before reposting or forwarding information to avoid unintentionally spreading falsehoods.

By equipping children with these skills, they become more informed and responsible digital citizens who can navigate the internet with confidence and discernment.

Encouraging Responsible Technology Use in Schools

Schools play a significant role in shaping children's relationship with technology. When used appropriately, digital tools enhance learning, creativity, and collaboration. However, without clear guidelines, excessive or inappropriate use of technology can become a distraction or even a risk. Encouraging responsible technology use in schools ensures that students maximize the benefits of digital learning while avoiding potential pitfalls.

The Importance of Responsible Tech Use in Schools

- **Enhances Learning** – Digital resources provide interactive and engaging ways to absorb information.
- **Develops Digital Literacy** – Students learn essential skills such as research, online safety, and ethical internet use.
- **Encourages Collaboration** – Online tools allow for teamwork and communication beyond the classroom.
- **Prepares for the Future** – Digital proficiency is essential for higher education and careers.

Steps to Promote Responsible Technology Use

- **Set Clear Guidelines** – Schools should establish digital policies outlining acceptable device use, appropriate websites, and consequences for misuse.
- **Teach Digital Literacy** – Include lessons on cyber safety, ethical online behavior, and evaluating information sources.

- **Monitor Device Usage** – Use classroom management software to track student activity and prevent distractions.
- **Encourage Balanced Use** – Promote a mix of screen-based and offline activities to prevent over-reliance on technology.
- **Limit Non-Educational Use** – Restrict access to social media, gaming, and entertainment websites during school hours.
- **Involve Parents** – Keep parents informed about their child's technology use and encourage at-home reinforcement of responsible habits.
- **Promote Ethical Online Behavior** – Encourage students to be respectful, thoughtful, and responsible when communicating online, whether in forums, emails, or collaborative projects.
- **Provide Alternative Learning Methods** – Ensure that students have access to non-digital learning tools to accommodate different learning styles.
- **Create a Culture of Accountability** – Encourage students to report inappropriate behavior, cyberbullying, or security concerns.

By fostering responsible technology use in schools, students can harness the power of digital tools while maintaining focus, discipline, and ethical behavior.

Conclusion

Raising tech-savvy and responsible digital citizens requires a collaborative effort between parents, educators, and children. By teaching ethical online behavior, helping kids navigate misinformation, and encouraging responsible technology use in schools, we can prepare the next generation to use digital resources wisely, safely, and respectfully. The goal is not to eliminate technology from children's lives but to empower them with the knowledge and skills needed to navigate the digital world responsibly and ethically.

Chapter 13: Preparing for the Future of Technology

Technology is evolving at an incredible pace, reshaping the way we live, work, and interact. For parents, understanding these changes is essential to guiding their children safely and wisely through the digital world. The rise of Artificial Intelligence (AI), Virtual Reality (VR), and the Metaverse is already influencing how kids learn, play, and communicate online. While these advancements bring exciting opportunities, they also introduce new challenges and risks.

In this chapter, we will explore the emerging technologies that are shaping the digital landscape, discuss how they will impact children's online experiences, and provide actionable steps for parents to prepare their kids for the future.

The Rise of AI, Virtual Reality, and the Metaverse

What is Artificial Intelligence (AI)?

Artificial Intelligence refers to computer systems that can perform tasks that typically require human intelligence. These tasks include understanding language, recognizing patterns, making decisions, and even learning from experience. AI is present in many aspects of daily life, from virtual assistants like Siri and Alexa to recommendation systems on YouTube and Netflix.

For children, AI is already shaping their digital experience in several ways:

- **Personalized Learning:** AI-powered apps adjust educational content based on a child's learning style and progress.
- **Chatbots & Virtual Assistants:** AI chatbots provide instant answers to kids' questions.
- **Automated Content Moderation:** AI helps filter out inappropriate content on social media and gaming platforms.

While AI enhances convenience and learning, it also raises concerns about **privacy, misinformation, and bias.** Parents need to understand how AI operates and educate their children about how to use it responsibly.

What is Virtual Reality (VR)?

Virtual Reality is a technology that creates immersive digital experiences. By wearing a VR headset, users feel as though they are inside a 3D world where they can interact with objects and characters. This technology is widely used in gaming, education, and even therapy.

How is VR affecting children?

- **Enhanced Learning:** Kids can explore historical events, outer space, or the deep ocean in VR.
- **Social Interactions:** Virtual reality chatrooms allow kids to interact with friends in digital spaces.
- **Gaming and Entertainment:** Many games now offer VR experiences that immerse children in fantasy worlds.

However, **VR also presents risks**, including motion sickness, eye strain, addiction, and exposure to inappropriate content. Supervision is essential to ensure safe and healthy use of VR technology.

What is the Metaverse?

The Metaverse is a digital universe where people interact through avatars in virtual environments. It combines elements of VR, augmented reality (AR), and the internet to create shared digital spaces.

How does the Metaverse impact children?

- **Virtual Socialization:** Kids can make friends and collaborate in virtual worlds.
- **Digital Economy:** Some games allow kids to buy, sell, and trade virtual goods.
- **New Learning Platforms:** Schools and educators are beginning to explore teaching in virtual classrooms.

While the Metaverse offers unique opportunities, parents should be aware of its potential **dangers, such as online predators, digital addiction, and privacy concerns.**

How Emerging Tech Will Change Kids' Online Experience

As AI, VR, and the Metaverse continue to grow, children's online experiences will become more immersive and interactive. Some key changes include:

More Personalized Online Content

- AI will tailor search results, videos, and educational materials to individual preferences.
- While this is beneficial, it can also create **filter bubbles** where kids are only exposed to information that aligns with their existing views.

Increased Digital Interaction

- Instead of typing or clicking, kids will increasingly interact using voice commands and gestures.
- The rise of AI-generated content means children may struggle to differentiate real from artificial.

The Expansion of Virtual Economies

- Kids will engage more in digital marketplaces where they can buy virtual items, currency, and NFTs.
- Parents should **teach financial responsibility** early to prevent unnecessary spending in digital worlds.

Blurring of Reality and Digital Spaces

- The line between the real world and digital life will continue to blur.
- Kids may spend more time in virtual spaces, making it essential to maintain **a balance between online and offline activities.**

Preparing Kids for Future Digital Trends

The best way to prepare children for these technological advancements is to **educate, supervise, and empower** them to use technology responsibly. Here are key steps parents can take:

1. Teach Digital Literacy and Critical Thinking

- Help children **understand AI** and how it influences the content they see.
- Encourage them to **question information online** and recognize fake news or AI-generated misinformation.
- Show them how to **identify online risks** in new digital spaces, such as deepfake videos and AI chatbots.

2. Set Boundaries and Screen Time Rules

- Establish **tech-free zones** at home, especially in bedrooms and during meals.
- Limit VR and screen time to **prevent overexposure** to digital worlds.
- Encourage kids to balance their time between **real-world activities and virtual engagement.**

3. Ensure Privacy and Security Awareness

- Teach children **not to share personal information** in virtual spaces.
- Use **privacy settings and parental controls** on AI-powered platforms, VR games, and the Metaverse.
- Discuss **the risks of data collection** and explain how companies track online behavior.

4. Encourage Healthy Online Social Interactions

- Teach kids about **digital etiquette** and how to communicate respectfully online.
- Warn them about **cyberbullying and online predators** in immersive digital environments.
- Encourage real-world friendships and outdoor activities to maintain a balanced lifestyle.

5. Introduce Kids to Future-Proof Skills

- Expose them to **STEM (Science, Technology, Engineering, and Math) activities** to build digital fluency.
- Teach basic coding or AI concepts to help them **understand and control technology** rather than just consuming it.
- Encourage creative skills such as **video editing, digital art, and game design**, which will be valuable in future careers.

Conclusion: Empowering Kids for a Digital Future

The future of technology is exciting, and while it brings many benefits, it also presents challenges that require proactive parenting. By staying informed about AI, Virtual Reality, and the Metaverse, parents can equip their children with the knowledge and skills they need to navigate the digital world safely and responsibly.

The key to preparing kids for the future is not to **shield them from technology** but to **teach them how to use it wisely.** With the right guidance, today's children can become tech-savvy, responsible digital citizens ready for whatever innovations the future holds.

Conclusion

The Role of Parents in Shaping Digital Behavior

As parents, our role in guiding and shaping our children's digital behavior cannot be overstated. The online world is an extension of our children's daily lives, just as real and impactful as the physical world. Just as we teach them how to behave respectfully, stay safe in public spaces, and make wise decisions in social situations, we must also equip them with the skills and mindset necessary to navigate the digital landscape responsibly.

Being a Digital Role Model

Children often learn more from what they see than what they are told. If we want them to use technology in a balanced, responsible, and ethical manner, we must first evaluate our own digital habits. Do we spend too much time on our phones? Do we engage in respectful discussions online? Do we practice good cybersecurity habits? These are all behaviors that children absorb and replicate.

As digital role models, we can:

- **Demonstrate healthy screen time habits** by balancing online and offline activities.
- **Practice respectful communication online** and encourage the same from our kids.

- **Show them the importance of digital privacy** by using strong passwords and being cautious with personal information.
- **Discuss responsible content sharing** and emphasize the lasting impact of their digital footprint.

Providing Guidance Without Being Overly Controlling

It's natural to want to protect our children from the many risks that exist online. However, being too strict or overly controlling may cause them to hide their online activities, making them even more vulnerable. Instead, we should strive to be approachable and involved, setting clear expectations while also allowing them to explore the digital world in a safe and age-appropriate manner.

Encouraging **open discussions, explaining risks instead of just forbidding things, and giving children the tools to make smart choices** will empower them to act responsibly even when we are not looking.

Final Digital Parenting Checklist

As a parent, keeping up with your child's digital activities can feel overwhelming at times. However, having a clear checklist to follow can help ensure you've covered the key aspects of digital parenting. This checklist serves as a practical guide to reinforce safe digital habits, set the right boundaries, and protect your child from online risks.

Digital Safety and Privacy

✓ Teach your child how to create and manage strong passwords.

✓ Enable two-factor authentication on all important accounts.

✓ Regularly review privacy settings on social media and apps.

✓ Educate your child about phishing scams and how to spot them.

✓ Discuss the importance of never sharing personal information online.

Healthy Digital Habits

✓ Set clear screen time rules and enforce healthy digital routines.

✓ Encourage a balance between online and offline activities.

✓ Avoid using devices during meals, family time, or bedtime.

✓ Model responsible technology use by practicing the habits you teach.

Safe Online Behavior

✓ Teach your child to recognize and report cyberbullying.

✓ Encourage them to think critically about what they read online.

✓ Discuss online predators and how to avoid suspicious interactions.

✓ Guide them on how to spot misinformation and fake news.

Parental Supervision and Monitoring

✓ Use parental controls where necessary, but maintain trust.

✓ Regularly check in on your child's online activities in an open and non-intrusive manner.

✓ Establish a **family digital agreement** to outline acceptable online behavior.

✓ Stay informed about new trends, apps, and online risks.

Emergency Preparedness

✓ Teach your child how to handle a hacked account.

✓ Show them how to block and report inappropriate content or users.

✓ Make sure they know who to turn to when facing online issues.

This checklist is not meant to be rigid but rather a flexible guide that can be adapted as your child grows and technology evolves.

Encouraging Open Communication About Online Safety

One of the most powerful tools in digital parenting is **open communication**. If children feel comfortable talking to their parents about their online experiences, they are more likely to seek guidance when they encounter challenges. Creating a judgment-free environment will encourage them to share their concerns instead of hiding them.

Building a Culture of Trust

- **Start early**: The sooner children understand that online safety is a normal topic of conversation, the more likely they will turn to you for advice.
- **Be approachable**: Let your child know they can talk to you about anything they see or experience online without fear of punishment or shame.

- **Listen without overreacting**: If your child admits to making a mistake online, react calmly and use it as a learning opportunity rather than a moment for discipline.
- **Ask open-ended questions**: Instead of just asking, "Did anything bad happen online?" try "What's something interesting you learned online today?" or "Have you ever seen anything that made you uncomfortable?"

Creating Safe Spaces for Digital Discussions

- Have regular **family check-ins** where everyone, including parents, shares something about their online experiences.
- Use **real-world examples** (news stories, documentaries, or personal experiences) to spark discussions about online risks.
- Encourage children to **think critically** by asking questions like, "How do you know if something online is true?"

Helping Children Handle Mistakes Online

No matter how much we prepare them, children will make mistakes online. Whether it's oversharing personal information, clicking on a scam link, or responding to an unkind comment, they need to know that mistakes are learning experiences, not reasons for shame.

If your child comes to you with an online mistake:

- **Stay calm** – They already feel bad and need guidance, not punishment.
- **Understand the situation** – Ask them to explain what happened.
- **Find a solution together** – Whether it's reporting a user, changing a password, or apologizing for a mistake, work through it as a team.

- **Use it as a learning opportunity** – Help them understand what they can do differently next time.

By encouraging **open, ongoing conversations** about digital safety, we empower children to become responsible digital citizens who can confidently navigate the online world while making smart, safe decisions.

Final Thoughts

Digital parenting is not about **controlling** every aspect of your child's online experience but about **guiding, teaching, and empowering** them to make responsible choices. The internet is an incredible tool that, when used correctly, can open doors to learning, creativity, and connection. By setting boundaries, educating children about risks, and maintaining open communication, we can create a safer, healthier digital world for the next generation.

As technology continues to evolve, so must our approach to parenting in the digital age. Staying informed, adaptable, and engaged in our children's online lives will ensure they grow into responsible, tech-savvy individuals.

Parenting in the digital world is not easy, but remember: **You are not alone.** Every small effort you make today will shape your child's future digital well-being.

Additional Resources

A s you navigate the journey of digital parenting, having the right tools and resources at your disposal can make a significant difference. This section provides two key resources:

- A **Parental Control Apps Comparison Chart** to help you evaluate and choose the best monitoring and safety tools for your family.
- A **List of Safe Websites & Apps for Kids** to ensure your child engages with age-appropriate, educational, and entertaining online platforms.

These resources will equip you with practical solutions to create a safer digital environment for your child.

Parental Control Apps Comparison Chart

Why Use Parental Control Apps?

The online world is vast, and while it offers endless opportunities for learning and entertainment, it also presents numerous risks. Parental control apps serve as an extra layer of protection, allowing you to:

- **Monitor Online Activity:** See which websites, apps, and content your child is accessing.
- **Set Time Limits:** Control screen time and prevent excessive device use.
- **Filter Inappropriate Content:** Block adult content, violence, and other harmful material.
- **Track Location:** Ensure your child's safety when they are outside the home.
- **Monitor Social Media & Messages:** Detect potential threats like cyberbullying or online predators.

However, not all parental control apps offer the same features, and some may be better suited for different needs. Below is a comparison chart to help you determine which app aligns with your family's requirements.

How to Use the Chart

Before diving into the comparison, consider these key questions:

- **What is my primary concern?** (Excessive screen time, inappropriate content, social media risks, online gaming, etc.)
- **What devices do we use?** (Some apps work better on iOS, Android, or PCs.)
- **What level of control do I want?** (Some apps offer strict monitoring, while others focus on education and guidance.)
- **What is my budget?** (Some parental control apps are free, while others require a subscription.)

Parental Control Apps Comparison Chart

Feature	Qustodio	Bark	Net Nanny	Norton Family	Google Family Link	Apple Screen Time
Content Filtering	✅ Yes	✅ Yes	✅ Yes	✅ Yes	✅ Yes (Limited)	✅ Yes (Limited)
Screen Time Limits	✅ Yes	✅ Yes	✅ Yes	✅ Yes	✅ Yes	✅ Yes
Social Media Monitoring	✅ Yes	✅ Yes (Extensive)	❌ No	❌ No	❌ No	❌ No
Text & Message Monitoring	❌ No	✅ Yes	❌ No	❌ No	❌ No	❌ No
Location Tracking	✅ Yes	✅ Yes	✅ Yes	✅ Yes	✅ Yes	✅ Yes
App & Website Blocking	✅ Yes	✅ Yes	✅ Yes	✅ Yes	✅ Yes	✅ Yes
Price (Per Month)	$4.58	$14	$4.99	$4.99	Free	Free

Choosing the Right App

Each of these apps has strengths and limitations. If social media monitoring is your biggest concern, **Bark** is a strong choice. For overall control, **Qustodio** and **Net Nanny** offer solid filtering and screen time management. If you prefer a free option, **Google Family Link** and **Apple Screen Time** provide basic controls.

By choosing an app that meets your needs, you can ensure that your child has a balanced and safe digital experience.

List of Safe Websites & Apps for Kids

Why It's Important to Curate Safe Digital Spaces

While the internet is full of educational and entertaining content, it also has a dark side. Many websites and apps contain inappropriate content, excessive advertisements, or hidden dangers like predators and scams. As a parent, guiding your child toward safe online spaces helps protect them while still allowing them to enjoy the benefits of digital learning and entertainment.

This list includes kid-friendly websites and apps that are:

✓ **Educational** – Promoting learning through fun activities.

✓ **Safe** – Free from harmful or inappropriate content.

✓ **Interactive** – Engaging with games, videos, and creative tools.

✓ **Age-Appropriate** – Designed with young users in mind.

Educational Websites & Apps

- **PBS Kids** (Website & App) – Fun educational games and videos for younger children.
- **Khan Academy Kids** (App) – Interactive lessons in math, science, and reading for preschool and elementary kids.
- **ABCmouse** (Website & App) – A subscription-based learning platform covering reading, math, and more.
- **National Geographic Kids** (Website) – Engaging articles, videos, and quizzes about nature and science.
- **Cool Math Games** (Website) – Fun math-based games for kids of all ages.
- **Duolingo Kids** (App) – A child-friendly version of Duolingo for learning new languages.

Entertainment & Creativity Websites & Apps

- **Toca Boca** (App) – Interactive digital toys that encourage creativity and storytelling.
- **Minecraft Education Edition** (App) – A classroom-friendly version of Minecraft for learning and creativity.

- **Scratch** (Website) – A coding platform where kids can create their own animations and games.
- **YouTube Kids** (App) – A safer version of YouTube with kid-friendly videos and parental controls.
- **Nickelodeon Games** (Website) – Fun, safe games based on popular Nickelodeon characters.
- **Lego Life** (App) – A safe social network for kids to share their Lego creations.

Safe Browsing Search Engines for Kids

- **Kiddle** – A child-friendly search engine powered by Google.
- **KidRex** – Another safe search engine that filters out inappropriate content.
- **Wacky Safe** – A web browser designed specifically for kids with filtered content.

How to Encourage Safe Browsing

Even with safe websites and apps, children should still be supervised. Here are some tips to encourage responsible online behavior:

- **Bookmark Safe Websites** – Set up a folder with pre-approved websites.
- **Use Parental Controls** – Enable restrictions on browsers and devices.
- **Educate About Online Safety** – Teach kids to avoid clicking suspicious links.
- **Encourage Offline Activities** – Balance screen time with real-world activities.

By guiding your child toward safe digital experiences, you help them build a positive and secure relationship with technology.

Final Thoughts

Parenting in the digital age can be challenging, but with the right tools and resources, you can create a safe and enriching online environment for your child. Use the parental control comparison chart to choose a monitoring solution that fits your family's needs. Additionally, encourage your child to explore educational and entertaining platforms that are designed with their safety in mind.

With informed decisions and proactive guidance, you can empower your child to be a responsible and tech-savvy digital citizen.

www.ingramcontent.com/pod-product-compliance
Lightning Source LLC
LaVergne TN
LVHW051736050326
832903LV00023B/943